MW01504469

MY GUARDIAN ANGEL
For Little Catholics

By Mary W. Stomwall
Edited by Bart Tesoriero

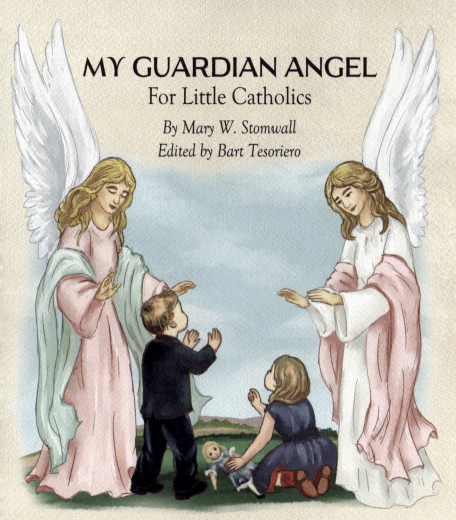

ISBN 978-1-61796-401-5
Artwork and Text © 2023 Aquinas Kids, Phoenix, Arizona
Printed in China

When you were born, many people gave you presents. Your Father in heaven gave you presents, too. One of God's many presents was your Guardian Angel. God said to him: "Here is someone especially important to Me. I want you to watch over this child always."

Your Guardian Angel was happy when you were baptized. He saw God's beauty come into you. Since then, your Angel has been trying to help you keep this beauty in your soul.

Your Guardian Angel is God's special friend. He loves God more than you do because he truly sees God all the time. He knows how much God loves us all.

Everybody in the world has a special Guardian
Angel. Even those who do not know God, or who
do not love or serve Him, have Guardian Angels.
That shows how much God loves us all.

You cannot see your Guardian Angel because he does not have a body.

You cannot see your thoughts either, but you know they are real. Your Angel never grows hungry or sleepy. He watches over you night and day.

Your Guardian Angel loves you very much. He sees God's life in you. He tells you to listen to God's voice in your soul. He reminds you to talk to God by praying.

Angels are often shown with wings. The wings help you to understand how quickly angels do the will of God.

Angels can go faster than a jet plane.

God made all the angels very beautiful. Some of them said, "Why should we obey God? We do not need Him, We are great enough," Those angels could not be in heaven, because everyone there loves God. Saint Michael the Archangel drove them into hell forever.

The bad angels became devils, because they would not love God. Now they try to make you do wrong things. That is why you need your Guardian Angel. He is strong, because God is always with him. Ask your Guardian Angel to help you do what is right.

When you play, your Guardian Angel reminds you to play fair. He tells you to be kind and gentle with other boys and girls. Your Angel knows that this is the best way to be happy.

When you pray, your Guardian Angel prays with you and for you. He carriers your prayers to God.

Your father and your mother have Guardian Angels too.

When your dad leaves for work, his Guardian Angel goes along to watch over him all day long.

When you go to Mass, your Guardian Angel kneels beside you. He really sees Our Lord when the priest holds up the Sacred Host. Ask your Guardian Angel to help you to know and love Jesus and the Mass.

When you are sick, you always have your Guardian Angel beside your bed.

Ask him to help you to suffer without complaining.

When you work at something hard, your Guardian Angel reminds you to do your very best because he wants you to do everything for the honor and glory of God.

Your Guardian Angel has a special day on October 2nd, the Feast of the Guardian Angels. The gift he most likes from you is to see you being extra good on this day and every day.

Besides Guardian Angels there are millions of other angels. They are always singing with joy before the throne of God in highest heaven. Day and night they praise and love and adore God.

Sometimes God gives these angels special work to do on earth. He sent the Archangel Gabriel to Mary. Gabriel told Mary that she was to be the Mother of Jesus. The Angel Gabriel is the patron saint of messengers, communication workers, and postal workers.

God sent the Archangel Raphael to help a boy named Tobiah on a long hard trip.

The boy's father was blind.

Raphael led Tobiah safely home, and then he cured the father's blindness.

God sent the Archangel Michael to tell Joan of Arc to save her country.

Saint Michael is also a very special Guardian Angel of the Church. Many Catholics pray the Prayer of Saint Michael after Mass.

The Guardian Angel of Portugal came to three children in Fatima. The Angel taught them this prayer.

"My God, I believe, I adore, I hope and I love You! I ask pardon for those who do not believe, do not adore, do not hope and do not love You."

Some people have really seen and talked with their Guardian Angels. When Saint Rose of Lima was a little girl, she sometimes gave her Guardian Angel special messages to take to Our Lord.

Saint Isidore worked for a farmer, but every day he went to Mass first. One morning, he saw his Guardian Angel

plowing a field for him. Then Isidore knew that God
was pleased with him.

Saint Zita had to bake bread early every morning.
Once she spent so much time praying that she forgot
to do her baking. When she hurried in, her Guardian
Angel was in the kitchen baking a fine loaf of bread
for her.

Prayer to Your Guardian Angel

Your Guardian Angel never leaves your side. He is with you night and day. He goes wherever you go. You are never alone.

Angel of God, My Guardian Dear,

Your Guardian Angel was given to you, because God loves you so much. Your Guardian Angel reminds you that God sees you all the time. God knows everything you think, say, or do!

To whom God's love commits me here.

Your Guardian Angel tells you to do good things.
He tries to keep your soul and body from harm.

Ever This Day Be at My Side,

Your Guardian Angel helps you if you listen to him. But he cannot make you do what is right and good. The more you listen to your Angel, the clearer and better you will understand what he wants you to do. And soon it will be easy for you to follow him all the way to heaven.

To Light and Guard, To Rule and Guide.

Angel of God, my guardian dear,
To whom God's love commits me here;
Ever this day be at my side,
To light and guard,
To rule and guide. Amen.

Some day you will see the full beauty of your Guardian Angel. You will also hear his voice when he leads you to God in heaven!